OPERA

OPERA

CLASSIC fM HANDY GUIDES

OPERA

ROB WEINBERG

First published 2015 by
Elliott and Thompson Limited
27 John Street
London WC1N 2BX
www.eandtbooks.com

ISBN: 978-1-78396-048-4

9 8 7 6 5 4 3 2 1

A catalogue record for this book is available from the British Library.

Typesetting: Marie Doherty
Printed in the UK by TJ International Ltd

Contents

Introduction

At Classic FM, we spend a lot of our time dreaming up wonderful ways of making sure that as many people as possible across the UK have the opportunity to listen to classical music. As the nation's biggest classical music radio station, we feel that we have a responsibility to share the world's greatest music as widely as we can.

Over the years, we have written a variety of classical music books in all sorts of shapes and sizes. But we have never put together a series of books quite like this.

This set of books covers a whole range of aspects of classical music. They are all written in Classic FM's friendly, accessible style and you can rest assured that they are packed full of facts about classical music. Read separately, each book gives you a handy snapshot of a particular subject area. Added together, the series combines to offer a more detailed insight into the full story of classical music. Along the way, we shall be paying particular attention to some of the key composers whose music we play most often on the radio station, as well as examining many of classical music's subgenres.

These books are relatively small in size, so they are not going to be encyclopedic in their level of detail; there are other books out there that do that much better than we could ever hope to. Instead, they are intended to be enjoyable introductory guides that will be particularly useful to listeners who are beginning their voyage of discovery through the rich and exciting world of classical music. Drawing on the research we have undertaken for many of our previous Classic FM books, they concentrate on information rather than theory because we want to make this series of books attractive and inviting to readers who are not necessarily familiar with the more complex aspects of musicology.

For more information on this series, take a look at our website: www.ClassicFM.com/handyguides.

Preface

Opera – to quote Dr Johnson – is an 'exotic and irrational entertainment', one that can elicit a wide range of responses from people. As with any form of music, you will find those who are so passionate about the genre that they spend their entire lives booking their holidays around performances and festivals; collecting, listening to and comparing recordings; and talking animatedly about every aspect of it with like-minded enthusiasts.

And at the other end of the spectrum, there are the ones who simply find it hard to take – or, at least, they say they do. Just hearing the word 'opera' spreads revulsion across their faces, their minds suddenly conjuring up the stereotypical image of a larger-than-life soprano, supposedly playing a consumptive teenager in her dying moments, managing to shriek at high pitch for several minutes.

Yet, between these two extremes are the football fans who still get goosebumps whenever they hear Pavarotti singing 'Nessun dorma'; the millions who vote on TV talent shows for a talented amateur with operatic aspirations; the summertime outdoor concert-goers who've tapped their feet along with 'La donna è mobile' while their smoked salmon sarnies turned to mush in a downpour; or the movie lovers whose breath was taken away by the use of a Mozart aria in *The Shawshank Redemption* or *The Ride of the Valkyries* booming out of helicopters over Vietnam in *Apocalypse Now*.

If you count yourself among any of the above, this book is for you. Consider it a small, assisted – and hopefully helpful – step into a sublime and often ridiculous art form, offering a taste of the many delights to be discovered.

one

Opera History in a Nutshell

The word 'opera' derives from the Italian term *opera in musica*, meaning 'work in music'. Having an Italian name, it's perhaps not surprising to learn that opera began during the Italian Renaissance a little more than 400 years ago.

Baroque Pioneers

The Baroque era lasted roughly from around 1600 to 1750. The earliest works emerged from the discussions of a group of brainy musicians, writers and noblemen, known as the Florentine Camerata. They were based in Florence and most of the music they came across consisted of either choral singing in a religious setting or very florid madrigals.

The Camerata wanted to revive the tradition of Greek theatre as they understood it to have been: sung rather than spoken. So they set out to combine music and text to tell gripping stories from classical mythology.

In 1597, one of their members, **Jacopo Peri** (1561–1633), wrote what is generally considered to be the first known opera, *Dafne*, in which he himself played the role of Apollo. It was a big success but hardly any music from it survives. Three years later, Peri composed another work, *Euridice*, based on the Greek legend that went on to become the subject of so many operas. It tells the story of heartbroken Orpheus venturing to Hades to retrieve his deceased wife Euridice. Peri's version was composed for the wedding of King Henry IV of France and his bride, Marie de' Medici of Florence. It's the earliest opera for which the score still exists today and already it's noticeable that Peri was experimenting with a new style of vocal delivery – something midway between speech and song where a solo voice was accompanied by simple chords played on a harpsichord or lute. This style of singing became known as *recitative* and the accompaniment as *continuo*.

As opera began to spread beyond Florence, it

found its first major practitioner in the person of **Claudio Monteverdi** (1567–1643), composer to the Duke of Mantua. Monteverdi's own version of the Orpheus story, *L'Orfeo*, premiered in 1607 and took opera to a new level of sophistication. In it the poetry and the music began to become equal partners. The protagonists were given real human feelings and characteristics, and orchestral instruments began to play a significant role. The *continuo* became more varied, perhaps plucked on strings or provided by an organ.

The first public opera house in Venice – the Teatro di San Cassiano – opened in 1637 and Monteverdi was commissioned to write a new work for it. *Adone* (1639) was such a hit that it ran continuously for six months. In 1642, his last and greatest work *L'incoronazione di Poppea* (*'The Coronation of Poppea'*) told the steamy story of the mistress of the Roman emperor Nero. Unlike other operas up to that point, *Poppea* was rooted in historical fact rather than legend. It also features one of opera's first stunning love duets, *'Pur ti miro'*, which nowadays is almost universally thought not to be by Monteverdi at all, but a colleague who worked on *Poppea* or one of its early revivals.

Thanks to the efforts of touring companies from Italy, opera began to spread throughout the rest of Europe. It took a while longer to catch on in France but, when it did, a different style evolved which combined the French nobility's passion for dance with simpler yet more expressive music. French opera's first great practitioner was **Jean-Baptiste Lully** (1632–1687), who was actually an Italian serving as the court composer for King Louis XIV. Lully's first opera, *Cadmus et Hermione* (1674), was a great success; the king was reportedly 'extraordinarily satisfied with this superb spectacle'. Lully pioneered special effects, made the dance an essential component of his works – much to the king's pleasure – and added ever more instruments to the opera orchestra. The Belgian film *Le Roi danse* (2000) brilliantly recreates the court of Louis XIV seen through the eyes of Lully.

A native Frenchman, **Jean-Philippe Rameau** (1683–1764) built on the foundations established by Lully. Rameau was already fifty when he wrote his first opera but went on to create many more. While retaining the use of classical myths, dance episodes and spectacular effects, Rameau approached his texts on a more human scale, making the music bring the emotional content to life. This dramatic intensity caused controversy among the circles that had been raised on Lully. *Hippolyte et Aricie* (1733) was acclaimed by many as bold and daring, but dismissed by others as 'turbulent' and 'a lot of noise'. Outraged Lullistes were worried that Rameau's growing popularity would oust their hero's music from the repertoire. They attacked Rameau's operas, while Ramistes hailed their man as the 'new Orpheus'. Long before the mods and rockers battled it out on Brighton's seafront, tension escalated between the two music fan factions throughout the 1730s. When Rameau's *Dardanus* opened in 1739, the composer was the subject of satirical engravings and a scurrilous poem, which resulted in physical violence.

Across the Channel, **Henry Purcell** (1659–1695) composed the first English opera, *Dido and Aeneas* (1689). He was commissioned to write it for a girls' school in London that had strong connections to the court and the London stage. The composer kept the opera short and easy to sing for his young performers. *Dido* told the story of the Queen of Carthage and her love for the heroic Aeneas from Troy. In general, however, English audiences in Purcell's day didn't have much of an appetite for opera; they preferred stage plays that included some musical elements and dance. Purcell's remarkable ability for setting words in a subtle way that communicated emotions was lost on London audiences whose passion for opera would not be ignited until Handel arrived in their midst, early in the following century.

But in the rest of Europe, by the end of the seventeenth and beginning of the eighteenth centuries, opera was hugely popular; there were some seventeen opera houses in Venice alone. Members of the nobility poured their money into creating opera companies and staging spectacular productions.

Two major styles emerged – *opera seria* (serious opera) and *opera buffa* (comic opera). The muscular exploits of Greek and Roman heroes came under the former category, the main narrative being carried by recitative while outbursts of passionate emotion were conveyed via vocal fireworks in show-off, show-stopping songs known as *arias*.

Opera buffa began in Naples as short comic interludes played out between the acts of an *opera seria* to give the audience light relief. *Buffa* works later evolved into operas in their own right. There were no heroic deeds of derring-do here; *buffa* told the stories of ordinary folk caught up in often farcical situations – but they still had to be able to sing like gods.

Indeed, as opera developed, the aria became the principal means by which a character could express his or her thoughts or feelings all the while showing off a formidable vocal technique. By the turn of the eighteenth century, opera audiences' main reason for attending was to see the stars of the day showing off their extraordinary vocal agility. The leading roles were usually sung by female sopranos and male castrati – men who had undergone a particularly unpleasant procedure while young to keep their voices high and pure. The greatest castrato was Farinelli (1705–1782), who was 'the acknowledged monarch of European singing'. Farinelli made a fortune, employed by King Philip V of Spain to sing the same four songs for him every night for twenty-five years.

In Venice, from around 1713, **Antonio Vivaldi** (1678–1741) – better known today as a composer of instrumental music, particularly *The Four Seasons* – devoted himself to opera and wrote more than forty of them. They are gradually being rediscovered today, although they are not notable for particularly advancing the genre. Meanwhile in Naples, **Giovanni Battista Pergolesi** (1710–1736) wrote one of the first, influential comic operas, *La serva padrona* (*'The Maid Mistress'*) in 1733, which told the story of how a maid fools her master into marrying her, thus becoming lady of the house. Pergolesi died far too young but left behind some innovative works, characterised by his mastery of melody, rhythm and witty writing for the voice.

The finest composer of *opera seria* was **George Frideric Handel** (1685–1759). In London, the nobility didn't bankroll opera; rather it was a commercial affair, performed by competing theatre companies. Handel arrived in London in 1710, his music having already established itself in people's affections from its use in a popular show at the Haymarket Theatre. His extravagant first London opera *Rinaldo* (1711) was widely acclaimed. The Haymarket became The King's Theatre and Handel's greatest operas were first staged there, attracting star names such as the sopranos Faustina Bordoni and Francesca Cuzzoni. The two *divas* had a bitter rivalry which erupted into a public riot in 1727 when audience catcalls and whistling led to the two of them exchanging real blows and pulling each other's hair during a production. Fans of the two singers threw chairs at each other. On another occasion, when Cuzzoni refused to sing an aria for Handel, the composer yelled at her, 'I well know that you are truly a She-Devil: but I will have you know that I am Beelzebub, chief of the Devils.' Handel threatened to dangle the singer upside down from a window until she agreed to perform.

Handel went further than any of his predecessors in going deeper into the emotional and psychological complexities of his characters. But the relative financial failure of his later operas convinced him that his path lay rather with oratorios, and it is for such masterpieces as *Messiah* (1741) that we know him best today.

The Age of Transition

In the second half of the eighteenth century, opera – along with so many other intellectual and artistic pursuits – underwent profound changes. Flamboyant heroic display made way for a more domestic-scale offering. Out went the unnecessary dances and vocal histrionics; in came arias, choruses and recitatives that truly served the drama.

Christoph Willibald Gluck (1714–1787) was vital to this transformation. He wrote more than forty operas, the most famous being *Orfeo ed Euridice* (1762). While the subject matter continued to draw on mythology, the way in which the characters behave is more naturalistic. For the first performance of *Alceste* (1767), Gluck went for actors who could sing rather than singers who would not be able to cope with the required level of authentic emotion. Gluck effectively set the seal on the Baroque era of opera and opened the way to the Classical era. His influence, though, would also be felt further down the years in the music of Richard Wagner and Richard Strauss, both of whom admired Gluck's work.

Wolfgang Amadeus Mozart (1756–1791) considered opera to be the supreme musical language, where everything was perfectly possible – and, naturally, he made it so. As with every other genre of music this genius touched, Mozart produced nothing but pure gold when it came to opera. He wrote his first stage work at the age of eleven and quickly went on to create several more with astounding confidence for one so young. His first masterpiece was *Idomeneo* (1781) which – while evidently influenced by Gluck – plays fast and loose with the *opera seria* conventions, effortlessly blending arias and recitative, and smoothly managing changes of scene and mood. Mozart brought to opera an unprecedented tunefulness, dazzling wit and an intense sense of drama, exploring such universal themes as love, fidelity and revenge. His final five operas – *The Marriage of Figaro* (1786), *Don Giovanni* (1787), *Così fan tutte* (1789), *The Magic Flute* (1791) and *La clemenza di Tito* (1791) – are nothing short of masterpieces, each of them a regular fixture in every opera company's repertoire today. One contemporary reporter who witnessed Mozart himself conducting a performance of *Figaro* from the keyboard said, 'Mozart directed the orchestra, playing his fortepiano; the joy which this music causes is so far removed from all sensuality that one cannot speak of it. Where could words be found that are worthy to describe such joy?'

The Italian Masters

With Gluck bringing a new naturalism into opera and Mozart blurring the lines between *seria* and *buffa*, the early nineteenth century saw the Italians, who originated the genre, looking for a saviour to take opera into a new era. He appeared in the form of **Gioachino Rossini** (1792–1868). Born the year after Mozart's untimely death, Rossini emerged as one of the greatest opera composers of all time and a pioneer of Romanticism. He rejuvenated both serious and comic opera with his superlative writing for the human voice, which regained its place as the dominant element in Italian opera. Audiences went wild at Rossini's melodies, and the range, speed and skill he demanded of singers. From comedies, such as the sparkling *The Barber of Seville* (1816) through to powerful melodramas such as *William Tell* (1829), Rossini's mastery of operatic form influenced composers throughout the entire continent. He wrote thirty-nine in total before happily retiring for the last four decades of his life.

The vocal brilliance that Rossini required from his performers, known as *bel canto* ('beautiful singing'), became the dominant genre of Italian Romantic opera. Two other Italian composers also came to be closely associated with this style.

Vincenzo Bellini (1801–1835) worked slowly, taking a lot of time over his handful of operas, carefully setting out to produce dramas that spoke to the emotions, and didn't just thrill the ear. Bellini's particular skill was to plunge deep into the human psyche, something that even the usually unimpressed Richard Wagner admired. Bellini was hugely successful, pretty much hitting gold straight away with his version of the 'Romeo and Juliet' story, *I Capuleti e i Montecchi* (1830), and *La sonnambula* (1831). Today his most popular and famous opera is *Norma* (1831), although it was not initially successful. It contains Bellini's most famous aria, *'Casta diva'*. 'I want something that is at the same time a prayer, an invocation, a threat, a delirium,' Bellini told his librettist. The composer's extremely long-flowing melodies earned him the nickname 'the Swan of Catania'.

At the other extreme, **Gaetano Donizetti** (1797–1848) composed more than seventy operas, although only a few still remain in the repertoire. In 1830, he had a major international success with *Anna Bolena*. Afterwards, his works were a mix of comedies such as *L'elisir d'amore* (1832) and intense dramas such as *Lucia di Lammermoor* (1835). Donizetti's operas are characterised by the extraordinary demands he makes on the singers. He also increased the role and range of the chorus, and innovated new types of song such as the *cavatina* – unhurried and melancholy – and the sensationally showy *cabaletta*.

The natural successor to Rossini, Bellini and Donizetti in the *bel canto* style was **Giuseppe Verdi** (1813–1901), the most successful opera composer ever. Over his long career, Verdi totally transformed the genre, experimenting with different musical and dramatic approaches to arrive at a unique, intensely melodramatic form of expression.

His first big success, *Nabucco* (1842), had an enormous impact, particularly with its *Chorus of the Hebrew Slaves* which caught the public imagination as an anthem for his country's liberation and bound Verdi to the movement for Italian unification. Twenty operas followed over the next seventeen years, the greatest of them being *Rigoletto* (1851), *Il trovatore* (1853) and *La traviata* (1853), today his most popular. Verdi's penultimate masterpiece, *Otello* (1877), is often considered the greatest Italian romantic opera, skilfully integrating solo arias, duets and choruses into the unfolding of the drama. Staying with his beloved Shakespeare, Verdi's final work, *Falstaff* (1893), broke all operatic conventions, discarding set pieces for a conversational flow of words that echoed ordinary speech. Today Verdi's works are among the most performed around the world and some of his tunes have become stand-alone hits, such as *'La donna è mobile'* from *Rigoletto*, the *Drinking Song* from *La traviata*, and the *Grand March* from *Aida* (1871).

Italian opera in the nineteenth century reached its peak as a complete fusion of all of the arts – drama, music, costume, stage design and effects. With Verdi, and later **Giacomo Puccini** (1858–1924), the story's psychological content became increasingly important. Puccini was the master of the *verismo* ('realism') style. *Verismo* first emerged in 1890 with Pietro Mascagni's short opera, *Cavalleria rusticana*. In its realistic – and sometimes violent – depiction of everyday happenings, *verismo* rejected the grand historical themes of Romanticism. In some of the most heartrending and passionate operas ever written, Puccini delved into the innermost thoughts and feelings of his characters, caught in difficult, intensely human situations. Most of his operas end in tragedy, usually for the women, so take lots of tissues. They include *Manon Lescaut* (1893), *La bohème* (1896), *Tosca* (1900), *Madama Butterfly* (1904) and *Turandot* (1926). Puccini's operas were, and remain, incredibly successful. The composer earned some $4 million from his works.

German Romantics

German operas in the seventeenth century had largely been *Singspiels,* which mixed spoken drama with musical interludes. Mozart brought new energy and a new seriousness to the genre with *The Magic Flute.* **Ludwig van Beethoven** (1770–1827) introduced lofty themes of justice, liberty and equality in his only opera, *Fidelio* (1805). In doing so, he produced a masterpiece that is one of the key works in the German repertoire. *Fidelio* initially wasn't such a success, however. The original performers moaned about the music and audiences found it too difficult. Beethoven revised the opera a number of times before arriving at a more successful version.

Another German, **Carl Maria von Weber** (1786–1826), was unhappy with the dominance in Europe of Italian operas and wanted to develop his own uniquely nationalistic approach. Weber's breakthrough was *Der Freischütz* (1821), in which he drew on Germanic folklore to tell the story of a marksman who makes a pact with the devil. Weber particularly sought to create a supernatural atmosphere by giving a dominant role to the orchestra. After its success, Weber went one stage further with *Euryanthe* (1823), in which he banished spoken dialogue altogether, blurred the boundary between recitative and aria, and produced a 'through-composed' opera.

Weber's approach was not lost on the young **Richard Wagner** (1813–1883), whose later innovations changed the course of music history. Wagner's big concept was that of the *Gesamtkunstwerk* (a 'complete work of art') in which music, poetry and visuals would all come together in one grandiose, total art form. Wagner even realised his dream of designing and creating a permanent home at Bayreuth where his works could be performed in the way he wanted. In his greatest works – *Tristan und Isolde* (1865), *Die Meistersinger von Nürnberg* (1868), the *Ring* Cycle (1869–76), and *Parsifal* (1882), Wagner gave opera a profound philosophical depth, often based on Germanic or Arthurian legends. The flow of music was dramatic, expansive, surging and seamless, giving a new prominence to the orchestra. Wagner also developed the concept of the *leitmotif*, a musical phrase connected to a specific person, place or idea, woven throughout the drama. *Die Meistersinger* wins the record for the longest single opera still performed today, usually coming in at around five hours and fifteen minutes.

It was hard for any German composer who came after Wagner to accommodate his innovations while finding a voice of his own. **Engelbert Humperdinck** (1854–1921), who worked as an assistant to Wagner at Bayreuth, did have success with *Hänsel und Gretel* (1893) which, while clearly influenced by his mentor, is an attractive and highly accomplished work.

Richard Strauss (1864–1949) was also strongly influenced by Wagner. Strauss's fifteen operas often include beautiful melodies and are usually included alongside other late German Romantics. But Strauss was also a revolutionary – listen to *Salome* (1905) or *Elektra* (1909) and you'll be shocked at their experimental and challenging sound. But his most famous and best-loved opera is among the most lushly romantic of them all. *Der Rosenkavalier* (1911) was a great success when it was first performed and has remained in the repertoire ever since. It owes as much to Mozart and the Viennese waltz as to Wagner's innovations. Significantly, Strauss particularly composed music that demanded great beauty and subtlety from the soprano voice. His notoriously demanding wife was a soprano.

Speaking of Vienna: in stark contrast to the weighty bombast of Wagner's innovations, the city of waltzes developed a lighter form of opera that won over people's hearts. Operetta was characterised by its appealing music, comic plots and spoken dialogue between the songs. The most popular example is *Die Fledermaus* (1874) by **Johann Strauss II** (1825–1899). *The Merry Widow* (1905) by **Franz Lehár** (1870–1948) was, and has remained, another big hit.

French Opera

By the end of the eighteenth century, serious French opera was in a poor state, with the innovations of Lully and Rameau consigned to history by the French Revolution. At this time, the Italian-born **Luigi Cherubini** (1760–1842) emerged, applying Gluck's principles to comic opera, giving it musical sophistication. Cherubini's works acted as a mirror to the turbulence of his times; his greatest, *Médée* (1797), reflects the bloodshed of the Revolution. It was a little too much for the French to handle, and became more popular abroad.

Rossini's final French opera, *William Tell* (1829), along with *La muette de Portici* (1828) by

Daniel Auber (1782–1871), signalled the birth of a new genre that dominated the French stage for the remainder of the nineteenth century: grand opera. These were works literally on a gigantic scale, inspired by historical subjects and involving vast numbers of performers, expanded orchestras, elaborate sets and costumes and lots of ballet. The most successful of grand-opera composers was the German-born **Giacomo Meyerbeer** (1791–1864). His *Robert le diable* (1831) was a massive success, with audiences particularly revelling in its ghoulish ballet danced by dead nuns rising from the grave. *Les Huguenots* (1836), *Le Prophète* (1849) and *L'Africaine* (1865) became firmly established in the repertoire, making Meyerbeer the most frequently performed composer around the world in the nineteenth century. He was also an early champion of Wagner, and instrumental in staging the first production of *Rienzi* (1842). But Wagner's later anti-Semitic attacks on Meyerbeer did lasting damage to the latter's enduring popularity.

A grand-opera composer whose works failed miserably in his own time but has seen a major revival in recent years is **Hector Berlioz** (1803–1869). Berlioz admired Rossini but was not a fan of the elaborate

Italian style. Seeking to create an opera that conveyed dramatic truth, Berlioz's first and only work for the Opéra National de Paris – *Benvenuto Cellini* (1838) – was a total flop. It took two decades before Berlioz began writing his masterpiece, *Les Troyens*, which was too ambitious for him ever to stage. Almost predicting how far ahead of his own time he was, Berlioz said, 'If only I could live till I am a hundred and forty, my life would become decidedly interesting.' His third and final opera, *Béatrice et Bénédict* (1862), based on Shakespeare's *Much Ado About Nothing*, was written for Germany, where his work was more appreciated than in his native France.

The opening of the Théâtre Lyrique in Paris in 1851 was instrumental in the emergence of a new generation of French opera composers. **Charles Gounod** (1818–1893) was interested in literary themes; his version of Goethe's *Faust* (1859) became one of the most frequently staged operas. **Georges Bizet** (1838–1875) did not enjoy much success in his own lifetime and died before *Carmen* (1875) became a worldwide smash. Its first audiences and critics were shocked by its violent realism and sensuality.

Jacques Offenbach (1819–1880) was unhappy

with the French operatic scene and wanted a venue where he could stage his own farces and satires, establishing his own small theatre. *Orpheus in the Underworld* (1858) parodied classical tragedy while mocking contemporary society. It was initially only a modest success but it soon benefited from an outraged newspaper review that condemned it for profanity and irreverence. The public flocked to see it and its scandalous 'can-can' dance. The great popularity of *Orpheus* prompted Offenbach to write more, including *La belle Hélène* (1864), *La vie parisienne* (1866), and the less frivolous *The Tales of Hoffmann* (1881).

Other French operas of the late nineteenth century included *Samson et Dalila* (1877) by **Camille Saint-Saëns** (1835–1921), and *Lakmé* (1883) by **Léo Delibes** (1836–1891). Its *Flower Duet* became a popular favourite after being revived in 1989 as the signature tune for British Airways. But by far the most successful composer of the time was **Jules Massenet** (1842–1912) who wrote twenty-five operas. Massenet was a master of melody. That meant most of his work did not survive into the twentieth century with its preference for atonality and dissonance. *Manon* (1884) and *Werther* (1892) have, however, regained popularity while the

Méditation interlude from his opera *Thaïs* (1894) remains a much-loved concert piece for violin and orchestra.

On the whole, though, French composers did not respond well to Wagner's innovations. *Pelléas et Mélisande* (1902) by **Claude Debussy** (1862–1918) was perhaps uniquely influenced by Wagner in the way that Debussy gave the orchestra a central role and abolished distinctions between aria and recitative altogether. Debussy felt there was 'too much singing' in opera and preferred instead to create a work where the voices reflected the rhythm of his native language.

Russian Nationalists

Opera arrived in Russia courtesy of Italian travelling players in the eighteenth century. While a few foreign composers serving in the Imperial Court dabbled with Russian-language operas, some native Russians tried their hand at writing works using Italian and French texts. It was these experiments that paved the way for the emergence of some outstanding Russian opera composers in the nineteenth century, who had a particularly strong relationship with the literature of their homeland.

The father of nationalist music in Russia was **Mikhail Glinka** (1804–1857). He combined authentic folk music, the singing of the Russian Orthodox liturgy, and traditional instruments such as the balalaika, to evolve an authentic Russian sound. Glinka's *A Life for the Tsar* (1836) was inspired by a true story about a peasant who gives up his life to protect the Tsar from an uprising. Along with *Russlan and Ludmilla* (1842) – based on a Pushkin fairy tale – Glinka's two operas established a new foundation on which Russian music could be built by the next generation.

The epic *Boris Godunov* (1874) by **Modest Mussorgsky** (1839–1881) remains Russian opera's greatest and most recorded masterpiece. Along with *A Life for the Tsar*, it's one of several operas that deal with complex themes from the country's history. But it's the only Russian work that has won for itself a lasting place in the repertoire – perhaps because of its psychological depth, not only of its eponymous protagonist but in Mussorgsky's presentation of the Russian people, who are given some of opera's most moving choruses, inspired by Orthodox chanting.

A Life for the Tsar also made a profound impact on the young **Pyotr Ilyich Tchaikovsky**

(1840–1893). He went on to complete ten operas, including the most famous, *Eugene Onegin* (1879), and *The Queen of Spades* (1890), both derived from works by Pushkin. *Onegin* is today the most popular of all Russian operas but it has a typically Western European sound. More traditionally Russian are the fifteen operas of **Nikolai Rimsky-Korsakov** (1844–1908), which offer excellent vocal writing and ingenious orchestral effects as in, for example, the well-loved *The Flight of the Bumblebee* from his opera *The Tale of Tsar Saltan* (1900). Rimsky-Korsakov's operas are exotic, poetic and more musical than they are dramatic. His fairy tale *The Golden Cockerel* (1909) is the most likely to be performed outside of Russia.

Alexander Borodin (1833–1887) worked as a highly successful chemist, and slotted his composing in during his leisure hours. He began working on his opera *Prince Igor* in September 1869 but soon began to have doubts and laid the work aside for years. He returned to it periodically but died suddenly, leaving it incomplete for Rimsky-Korsakov to finish. *Igor* is best known today for its colourful Polovtsian Dances orchestral and choral sequence.

In the early twentieth century, Russia's political

turmoil posed particular challenges for those composers who attempted to work under the restraints
of the Soviet regime. **Dmitri Shostakovich** (1906–
1975) struggled for all of his life to operate within
the Communist ideology. His second opera, *Lady
Macbeth of the Mtsensk District* (1934), was harshly
condemned by the Soviet authorities; it's possible
that Stalin himself wrote a scathing review of the
opera in the *Pravda* newspaper.

A twentieth-century composer who spent much
time outside of Russia but later came under fire
from the regime when he returned was **Sergei
Prokofiev** (1891–1953). Opera was Prokofiev's
greatest interest and he produced twelve, including *The Gambler* (1917) and *The Fiery Angel* (1955),
which premiered after his death. The one relative
success during his lifetime was *The Love for Three
Oranges* (1921), written for Chicago Opera and subsequently performed over the following decade in
Europe and Russia.

Igor Stravinsky (1882–1971) spent most of
his composing career outside Russia and brought
his revolutionary approach to music into the opera
house as well as to the ballet stage and concert hall.
In 1951, his work *The Rake's Progress*, with a libretto

by W. H. Auden, was premiered in Venice, before being staged around Europe and at the New York Metropolitan Opera. *The Rake's Progress*, though, can hardly be called a Russian opera; its music is the finest example of Stravinsky's move into composing in a neo-classical style.

The Czechs

In the nineteenth century, opera became part of the development of a musical style that was to be identified with the aspirations of the Czech people for independence from the German-speaking Habsburg dynasty. A pioneer in this movement was **Bedřich Smetana** (1824–1884), Czechoslovakia's first nationalist opera composer. Before Smetana, Czech national opera had consisted only of a number of rarely performed works. In his second and most famous opera, *The Bartered Bride* (1866), Smetana used melodies and rhythms from Bohemian folk songs and dances in his quest to create an authentic Czech form of opera.

Antonín Dvořák (1841–1904) took nationalism a stage further and believed that opera was 'the most suitable form for the nation'. He had played viola in the works of Meyerbeer while an orchestral member in Prague and wanted to find a style that combined Meyerbeer's grand vision with Czech nationalist sentiment. Of his ten operas, only Dvořák's *Rusalka*, containing the well-loved *Song to the Moon*, is regularly performed these days.

For the early part of his career, **Leoš Janáček** (1854–1928)˙ was heavily influenced by Dvořák and it wasn't until Janáček was in his sixties that he evolved a highly personal, modern voice that drew on elements of folk music, portraying a greater realism and connection with everyday life. His operas in particular demonstrate the use of speech-derived melodic lines. The success of his first opera *Jenůfa* (1904) – which took him ten years to write – opened the doors to the world's opera stages for Janáček. In his twilight years, he produced his greatest works, including *Káťa Kabanová* (1921), *The Cunning Little Vixen* (1924) and *The Makropulos Case* (1926) – works that established him for all time as one of the most important Czech composers.

Modern Masters

As with other musical genres, opera composers in the early twentieth century made a conscious move away from melody and harmony to embrace dissonance to express extreme emotions and the existential crises of the age. It began with Wagner, to be followed by Richard Strauss, Debussy, Puccini in his final opera, *Turandot*, and was then carried through by truly modernist composers such as Berg and Britten.

Alban Berg (1885–1935) wrote just two operas – *Wozzeck* (1925) and the unfinished *Lulu* (1928–35). Discordant and shockingly dramatic, the operas of Berg had a profound influence on the composers that followed. In *Wozzeck*, the story of a murderer, Berg introduces the notion that an opera's protagonist can be flawed and tragic, and treated with sympathy and dignity. *Lulu* is concerned with obsession, forbidden desires and violence.

The Hungarian **Béla Bartók** (1881–1945) composed one opera, which is just an hour or so long. But *Duke Bluebeard's Castle* (1918) is a masterpiece. It is dark, brooding and expressionistic, with moments of magical transcendence. In it Bartók presents the rhythms and tonality of his native folk music, combined with the influence of Wagner, Richard Strauss, Ravel and Debussy. The major contribution made by Frenchman **Francis Poulenc** (1899–1963) to the operatic repertoire is *Dialogues des Carmélites* (1957). Its climax, in which the chorus of nuns fades away to a single voice as each of them in turn faces the guillotine, is a stunning *coup de théâtre*.

In the first decades of the twentieth century, a distinctive form of musical theatre also began to emerge across the Atlantic in the United States, pioneered largely by immigrants from Europe. By the late 1930s, stage musicals began to be written with a more operatic structure and included complex writing for voices. A graduate of 'Tin Pan Alley' and Broadway, **George Gershwin** (1898–1937) described his *Porgy and Bess* (1935) as a folk opera, and it's only in recent decades that it has become a seriously recognised addition to the repertoire of most of the world's opera houses. Incorporating stylistic elements of jazz, spirituals, blues and popular songs, *Porgy* was hugely ambitious and not immediately popular. But its songs have become standards for singers in all genres.

Also in the United States, the charismatic conductor, composer, pianist and educator, **Leonard Bernstein** (1918–1990) revolutionised music theatre in 1957 with *West Side Story* – arguably operatic in its dramatic scope and musical sophistication, but quintessentially Broadway with its thrilling dance numbers and jazz influences. Bernstein's operetta *Candide* (1956) got off to a problematic start but subsequently emerged, after extensive revisions, as an accomplished work in its own right, filled with scintillating, often witty music and a winning overture that is a favourite in concert halls.

In England, **Benjamin Britten** (1913–1976) lived on and around the Suffolk coast and much of his best work brilliantly evokes the relationship between man, society and nature. With *Peter Grimes* (1945), the story of an anti-hero in the mould of *Wozzeck*, Britten singlehandedly revived English opera, a genre that had been dormant since the time of Purcell. Britten went on to write several other powerful, often darkly dramatic, operas – among them *Billy Budd* (1951), *The Turn of the Screw* (1954) and *Death in Venice* (1973). His contemporaries William Walton (1902–1983) and Michael Tippett (1905–1998) also tried their hand at opera with more limited success.

From the late twentieth century until today, opera has continued to be a hugely expensive art form. A staple diet of Mozart, Verdi, Puccini and Bizet's *Carmen* continues to keep most of the major opera houses in business – and it is not always viable to stage new works without suffering considerable losses. A few contemporary composers, however, have managed to buck the trend and attract audiences, particularly younger people, to new works.

The hypnotic, repetitive and brooding minimalism of **Philip Glass** (born in 1937) has worked well on the stage, especially when the composer has collaborated with a director and a choreographer who can echo the construction and patterns of the music. Glass's 'portrait opera trilogy' began with the plot-free *Einstein on the Beach* (1975), which interpreted various aspects of the great scientist's life and work in music and movement. *Satyagraha* (1980) was based on the early experiences of Mahatma Gandhi in South Africa, while *Akhnaten* (1984), about the Egyptian pharaoh, was sung in ancient languages. Glass has gone on to write less captivating operas about other important historical figures including Columbus, Galileo and Walt Disney.

Another American, **John Adams** (born in 1947) has enjoyed considerable success with his operas, particularly *Nixon in China* (1987) and *The Death of Klinghoffer* (1991). Eschewing stories from mythology or the distant past, Adams draws on real-life modern subjects. *Nixon in China* toured the US in the late 1980s and won widespread popular acclaim. *Klinghoffer* is the story of the 1985 hijacking by Palestinians of the cruise ship *Achille Lauro* and the killing of an American passenger.

Today, CDs, downloadable tracks, gala concerts and the broadcasting of live performances into cinemas around the world have all made great opera more accessible than ever before. The most popular arias – dating all the way back to Purcell, Gluck and Monteverdi – appear on compilation albums, while a number of singers enjoy the kind of celebrity and acclaim usually reserved for their counterparts in the pop world. Whether any newly written operas, however, will stand the test of time and become classics that will be performed hundreds of years from now, or whether there is a composer yet to be born who can take opera into a new stage of development, as Mozart, Verdi or Wagner once did, still remains to be seen.

Whatever the future holds, there is – in the meantime – more than 400 years of beautiful and thrilling music from operas to be discovered and enjoyed.

two

The Men Behind
the Words

Even if an opera is based on classical mythology, or works by Shakespeare or Pushkin, it
still needs someone to provide a text that a composer can work with. The librettist is the person
who writes the words for operas and should, there-
fore, be given due credit as a major contributor to
the success of a piece. Here are a few of the great
librettists:

Metastasio (1698–1782)
Metastasio was one of Europe's most celebrated
opera seria librettists; his words were set by many
composers. Well suited for virtuoso sopranos and
castrati, his work fell out of fashion as opera became

less florid and moved towards more human, psychological interests.

Lorenzo da Ponte (1749–1838)

The Venetian poet and librettist wrote the words
for twenty-eight operas by eleven different composers, including three Mozart masterpieces – *Don
Giovanni*, *The Marriage of Figaro* and *Così fan tutte*.
Da Ponte's own colourful life is well worth reading
about; it could be the subject of an opera in its own
right.

Ludovic Halévy (1834–1908) and Henri Meilhac (1831–1897)

This French duo wrote a large number of libretti,
including their most famous collaboration on Bizet's
Carmen. For Offenbach, they also wrote – among
others – *La belle Hélène* and *La vie parisienne*.

Arrigo Boito (1842–1918)

Boito is best remembered today for providing
the words to Verdi's *Otello* and *Falstaff*, although
the duo's efforts to turn *King Lear* into an opera
never came to fruition. He also wrote the libretto
for *La Gioconda* (1876) by Amilcare Ponchielli

(1834–1886). Boito's own opera *Mefistofele* is itself full of sublime music.

Hugo von Hofmannsthal (1874–1929)

The Austrian writer struck up a particularly successful relationship with Richard Strauss and provided several libretti, including *Elektra* and *Der Rosenkavalier*.

W. H. Auden (1907–1973)

The Anglo-American poet wrote the words for, among other works, *Paul Bunyan* (1941) by Britten, and Stravinsky's *The Rake's Progress*. He also worked on a new translation of *The Magic Flute*, adding dialogue and re-ordering its scenes to create greater dramatic coherence.

Some other, perhaps unexpected, figures that have contributed libretti to operas include: **Hans Christian Andersen** (1805–1875), the fairy-tale author, who penned the texts to four Danish operas; **Charles Dickens** (1812–1870), who wrote the words for his friend John Pyke Hullah's *The Village Coquettes*; **Frederick the Great of Prussia** (1712–1786) who presented the Kapellmeister of

the Berlin Opera with the libretti for four works;
E. M. Forster (1879–1970), the English author,
who collaborated on the libretto for Britten's *Billy
Budd*, and **Francis Burdett Money-Coutts**
(1852–1923), a London banker who became patron
to the composer **Isaac Albéniz** (1860–1909) on
condition that Albéniz used Money-Coutts's own
libretti for his operas.

three

Operatic Voices

More than anything else for an opera audience, it is the voice of an exceptional singer that prompts the most excitement. Singers can reach such heights of popularity that they acquire a nickname that captures their brilliance: Maria Callas (1923–1977) became known as 'La Divina', Joan Sutherland (1926–2010) as 'La Stupenda', Jenny Lind (1820–1887) as the 'Swedish Nightingale' and the Italian baritone Titta Ruffo (1877–1953) as 'Voice of the Lion'.

Most voices of whatever quality can be classified under seven major categories, decided by the range of notes that the voice can encompass. Women's voices are usually either soprano, mezzo-soprano or contralto; men divide into four groups: countertenor, tenor, baritone and bass.

Soprano

The highest female vocal range, there are several different kinds of soprano voice, for example: the lyric *coloratura* that can manage a role such as Gilda in *Rigoletto* or Lucia di Lammermoor, or a dramatic *coloratura* capable of ornamentation, such as Callas or Sutherland. A *soubrette* has a light, pretty voice for Mozart roles such as Susanna in *The Marriage of Figaro* or Zerlina in *Don Giovanni*. A *spinto* must be able to push her lighter voice at times to create a bigger sound, particularly in roles such as Madama Butterfly or Tosca. Wagnerian sopranos are the real belters, able to meet the ferocious demands of such roles as Brünnhilde or Isolde. Other legendary sopranos have included Birgit Nilsson (1918–2005), Victoria de los Ángeles (1923–2005), Leontyne Price (born in 1927), Montserrat Caballé (born in 1933) and Lucia Popp (1939–1993).

Mezzo-soprano and Contralto

The mezzo-soprano voice sits between soprano and contralto. Its range is close to the soprano but without the very highest notes, and the tone is usually heavier and darker. These days, most contralto voices are also referred to as mezzo except for very low voices, suitable for such roles as Ulrica in Verdi's *A Masked Ball* (1859). A lyric mezzo voice would be suitable for the character of Carmen, Octavian in *Der Rosenkavalier* or Cherubino in *Figaro*. Such singers include Janet Baker (born in 1933) or Anne Sofie von Otter (born in 1955). A coloratura mezzo can manage vocal fireworks – think of Cecilia Bartoli (born in 1966) or the character Rosina in *The Barber of Seville*.

Countertenor

The use of high adult male voices was common in all-male choirs as early as the mid-sixteenth century. In the second half of the twentieth century, the countertenor voice became very popular again, partly because of the revival of Baroque opera with male roles written originally for castrati. Some modern operas, particularly those of Britten, included leading parts for countertenors. The title role in Philip Glass's *Akhnaten* is also played by a countertenor. Outstanding countertenors have included Alfred Deller (1912–1979), James Bowman (born in 1941) and Andreas Scholl (born in 1967).

Tenor

The tenor voice got its name in the Middle Ages when the job of the tenor was to 'hold' (Latin: *tenere*) the tune while the other voices provided the harmonies. Outstanding tenors include Jussi Björling (1911–1960), Luciano Pavarotti (1935–2007), José Carreras (born in 1946), Roberto Alagna (born in 1963), Jonas Kaufmann (born in 1969), Juan Diego Flórez (born in 1973) and Joseph Calleja (born in 1978). The voice of Plácido Domingo (born in 1941) has become lower in his senior years and this erstwhile member of the Three Tenors (the other two were Carreras and Pavarotti) is now a baritone.

Baritone

The baritone voice sits in the middle of the three male vocal ranges – between tenor and bass. Until the early nineteenth century, any male singer who was not a tenor was called a bass. The baritone designation then evolved, particularly in Germany. Lyric baritone voices – for roles such as Marcello in *La bohème* – include Dietrich Fischer-Dieskau (1925–2012), Thomas Allen (born in 1944) and Simon Keenlyside (born in 1959). A *kavalierbariton* can cope with both lyric and dramatic roles, such as Iago in Verdi's *Otello*. Such singers include Eberhard Wächter (1929–1992) and Leo Nucci (born in 1942). A *charakterbariton* suits Verdian roles, requiring a powerful, flexible voice – such as Tito Gobbi (1913–1984) and Sherill Milnes (born in 1935).

Bass

Derived from the Italian word *basso* ('low'), this is the lowest male voice. As with the other ranges, different kinds of basses have evolved to tackle a range of roles. A *spielbass* or *bassbuffo*, for example, is a lyrical voice that can cope with comic acting too, for roles such as Donizetti's Don Pasquale; a good example is the English singer Andrew Shore (born in 1952). A *basso profondo* is a deep and powerful voice that can sing such parts as Mussorgsky's Boris Godunov or Mozart's Sarastro in *The Magic Flute*. Singers with this kind of voice have included the legends Feodor Chaliapin (1873–1938) and Boris Christoff (1914–1993).

four

Where to See Opera

If your only exposure to opera is hearing one of the more popular tunes from *Carmen*, *La traviata* or *La bohème* on the radio or at an open-air gala, the first thing to say is that there is a whole lot more to seeing the performance of a complete opera. There will be dramatic, maybe melodramatic, acting and extremely engrossing – and usually unbelievable – plots; stirring choruses; exotic dancing (perhaps); the awe-inspiring spectacle of sets, costumes, lighting and visual effects; and the full-on power of a symphony orchestra. So many creative elements and talents combine in an opera to give the audience an unforgettable experience.

It is not difficult to see live opera – and it is not always prohibitively expensive either. In addition to the major national companies, opera productions are almost always touring around regional and local theatres in the United Kingdom. There are often visually stunning arena shows at London's Royal Albert Hall or open-air performances in the summer at various country houses and historic locations. World-class productions are now screened regularly in local cinemas.

Here is a comprehensive list of companies putting on operas in the United Kingdom and around the world.

Major UK Companies

English National Opera (ENO)

Resident at the London Coliseum in St Martin's Lane, ENO presents a varied and exciting range of innovative productions – of both classics and contemporary opera – sung in English.

Website: www.eno.org

Glyndebourne Festival Opera

The East Sussex country house has had its own festival since 1934. This is the full-on experience

– beautiful setting, formal dress, long intervals for dining, and superb performances in the purpose-built opera house. After the season, Glyndebourne Touring Opera takes productions around the UK.

Website: www.glyndebourne.com

Royal Opera House, Covent Garden

This historic stage has welcomed such legends as Callas, Domingo, Pavarotti, Sutherland and Kiri Te Kanawa (born in 1944). Under current Musical Director Sir Antonio Pappano (born in 1959), the company continues to present world-class productions with the greatest contemporary singers.

Website: www.roh.org.uk

Opera North

Based at the Leeds Grand Theatre, this exciting regional company presents regular seasons in Nottingham, Salford Quays and Newcastle-upon-Tyne, performed either in English or in the original languages. The Orchestra of Opera North is Classic FM's Orchestra in Yorkshire.

Website: www.operanorth.co.uk

Scottish Opera

Scotland's award-winning national opera company was founded in 1962. Based in Glasgow, it takes its productions to Edinburgh, Inverness, Aberdeen and as far afield as the Scottish islands.

Website: www.scottishopera.org.uk

Welsh National Opera (WNO)

Founded in 1946, WNO tours extensively, giving regular performances in Cardiff, Llandudno and Swansea in Wales, and Bristol, Birmingham, Liverpool, Milton Keynes, Oxford, Plymouth and Southampton in England.

Website: www.wno.org.uk

Other UK Companies

English Touring Opera (ETO)

The leading touring opera company in the UK, ETO tours to more than 50 venues and presents as many as 110 performances each year.

Website: www.englishtouringopera.org.uk

Garsington Opera

Performances of high artistic quality in a spectacular Opera Pavilion at Wormsley, set within the rolling landscape of the Chiltern Hills.

Website: www.garsingtonopera.org

Grange Park Opera

A summer season of four productions staged in a 550-seat state-of-the-art theatre near Winchester.

Website: www.grangeparkopera.co.uk

Opera Holland Park

An annual summer programme of performances staged in a 1000-seater auditorium in Kensington, London. Around half a dozen operas are presented each summer, including adventurous productions of little-known works.

Website: www.rbkc.gov.uk/subsites/
operahollandpark.aspx

International

Opera Australia

Australia's principal opera company performs at the iconic Sydney Opera House for some eight months of the year, with the rest of its time spent at the Arts Centre Melbourne.

Website: www.opera.org.au

Vienna State Opera, Austria

Dating back to the mid-nineteenth century, the Vienna State Opera stages the world's greatest operas. Immediately before each performance, cheap, standing-room tickets are sold.

Website: www.wiener-staatsoper.at

La Monnaie, Belgium

The National Opera of Belgium takes the name of the Brussels theatre in which it is housed. Among the many significant premieres that have taken place here are Massenet's *Hérodiade*, Prokofiev's *The Gambler* and John Adams's *The Death of Klinghoffer*.

Website: www.lamonnaie.be/en/

Opéra National de Paris, France

Inaugurated in 1989, the magnificent modern Opéra Bastille seats 3,000 and, alongside the sumptuous Palais Garnier, is home to the Opéra National de Paris. Most operas are staged at the Bastille, along with some ballet and symphony concerts, while the Garnier presents a mixture of opera and ballet.

Website: www.operadeparis.fr

Opéra National de Lyon, France

This significant company has given some important French premieres of major operas, including Wagner's *Die Meistersinger* in 1896 and Mussorgsky's *Boris Godunov* in 1913. The first staged performance of Schoenberg's *Erwartung* took place here in 1967. Past principal conductors at the company have included John Eliot Gardiner (born in 1943) and Kent Nagano (born in 1951).

Website: www.opera-lyon.com

Bayreuth Festival, Germany

One for the serious Wagner enthusiasts only. The composer himself conceived and promoted the idea of a special festival to showcase his own works. Performances take place in the Festspielhaus, the design and construction of which was personally supervised by the composer. Expect to wait years to obtain tickets.

Website: www.bayreuther-festspiele.de/

The Deutsche Oper am Rhein, Germany

Since 1956, the Deutsche Oper am Rhein has performed both in the opera house in Düsseldorf and the theatre in Duisburg. The opera also has an associated ballet company.

Website: www.operamrhein.de

Deutsche Oper Berlin, Germany

The Deutsche Oper Berlin performs in Germany's second largest opera house. General music directors of the company have included such legendary conductors as Bruno Walter (1876–1962) and Lorin Maazel (1930–2014).

Website: www.deutscheoperberlin.de

Komische Oper Berlin, Germany

This company specialises in German-language productions of opera, operetta and musicals. It is located on Behrenstrasse, just a few steps from the famous Berlin street Unter den Linden.

Website: www.komische-oper-berlin.de

La Scala, Italy

One of the world's legendary opera houses. Most of the world's greatest operatic artists have appeared here during the past 200 years.

Website: www.teatroallascala.org/en

Teatro La Fenice, Italy

One of the most famous theatres in Europe, the site of many famous operatic premieres. Its name – The Phoenix – reflects its role in permitting an opera company to 'rise from the ashes'; since opening and being named La Fenice, it has burned down and been rebuilt twice.

Website: www.teatrolafenice.it

The Bolshoi, Russia

Moscow's historic theatre specialises in the giants of Russian opera, including Mussorgsky, Glinka, Rimsky-Korsakov and Tchaikovsky. Many of the productions are on a grand scale, with huge casts and dancers on stage for crowd scenes.

Website: www.bolshoi.ru/en/persons/opera/

Mariinsky Theatre, Russia

This historic theatre (formerly the Kirov) in St Petersburg opened in 1860 and became the pre-eminent music theatre of late nineteenth-century Russia, where many of the nation's masterpieces received their premieres. Since 1988, the conductor Valery Gergiev (born in 1953) has served as the general director.

Website: www.mariinsky.ru/en

The Cape Town Opera, South Africa

South Africa's largest performing arts organisation and the only opera house in Africa with a year-round programme. The company produces many fully staged operas during its annual season at the Opera House of the Artscape Theatre Centre, the Baxter Theatre Centre, the Joseph Stone Auditorium and some fifteen other venues throughout South Africa.

Website: www.capetownopera.co.za

Oper Zürich, Switzerland

Oper Zürich gives performances in the Opernhaus Zürich which has been the company's home for fifty years. It has been the setting for numerous world premieres, such as Berg's *Lulu*.

Website: www.opernhaus.ch/en/

The Dallas Opera, US

The Dallas Opera performs at the city's AT&T Performing Arts Center. The company often attracts world-class singers for the classic repertoire and stages many new commissions.

Website: http://dallasopera.org

Los Angeles Opera, US

America's fourth-largest opera company is led by Plácido Domingo, who has sung twenty-four different roles with them. He has also conducted thirteen operas and numerous concerts here.

Website: www.laopera.org

Lyric Opera of Chicago, US

One of the great international companies, the Lyric Opera of Chicago is renowned around the world for its artistic excellence, attracting the very finest singers every season for operas and concerts.

Website: www.lyricopera.org/

Metropolitan Opera, US

The Met is located at the Lincoln Center for the Performing Arts in New York City and presents around twenty-seven different operas each year in a season that lasts from late September to May.

Website: www.metopera.org

five

What To Do at the Opera

A night at the opera can be an unforgettable experience but it might also be a little daunting for the first-timer. Here are a few, hopefully helpful, tips if you are new to live opera performances:

Before the Show Begins ...

It's a good idea to read and become familiar with the synopsis of the opera you are about to see before it gets under way. Even with the libretto translated for you in surtitles, it can make it more enjoyable if you know what's going to happen in advance – but don't read through to the end of the synopsis if you don't want the end to be spoiled.

It's not really necessary to dress up these days for most opera performances although, if you are uncertain, it might be a good idea to check in advance with the venue. Some of the more upmarket summer festivals do expect black tie.

Make sure you have attended to the call of nature before the opera begins. The people behind and beside you won't take too kindly to your getting up and clambering over them once the show is under way.

Get to your seat before the curtain goes up and get yourself comfortable before the overture starts.

Turn off your mobile phone, alarm watch and any other electronic device that might arouse the fury of your fellow audience members (and indeed the performers).

Should you be prone to dozing off in a darkened auditorium and snoring loudly, request your companion in advance to elbow you in the ribs.

Once the Opera Has Started ...

Try to refrain from unwrapping particularly scrunchy sweet wrappers or noisily sharing other confectionery with your companions.

Refrain from talking during the performance. It is however permissible to clap/cheer/shout 'Bravo!' (for the chaps) and 'Brava!' (for the ladies) at the end of a brilliantly performed aria. If in doubt, just see what everyone else does and follow suit.

Do not sing or hum along if there's a tune you recognise.

Allow yourself to believe the story as it is told on stage; suspension of disbelief is an important element of opera.

Listen and watch carefully and let your emotions respond – although loud sobbing could distract your neighbours.

Some people like to select their favourite character or singer and watch that performer closely. You might want to identify what makes a particular singer stand out.

six

—

40 Essential Operas

Even the most devoted of opera buffs could not possibly like every single opera. As we have seen, the history of the genre ranges across centuries of changing musical styles and fashions. And there's the full gamut of human experience contained within operatic works – from light and frivolous comedy to intense, psychological drama.

So here's an introductory suggestion of forty works (listed alphabetically by composer) in the hope you will find something to like.

Ludwig van Beethoven: *Fidelio* (1805)

Beethoven's only opera is one of the greatest, a testament to the composer's passion for human liberty.

It's the story of a loyal wife who enters into a prison, disguised as a boy, to rescue her husband.

Knockout moment: *'O welche lust'* ('O what a joy') – the chorus sung by the prisoners as they emerge from their dungeon into dazzling light.

Vincenzo Bellini: *Norma* (1831)

In this tragedy set in occupied Gaul, the druid priestess Norma is urged to inspire a rebellion against the Romans. But she has two sons by a secret lover – a Roman official. Predictably, it doesn't end well.

Knockout moment: *'Casta Diva'* ('Chaste Goddess') sung by Norma, praying for peace to be spread over the land. Bellini rewrote this aria some eight times.

Hector Berlioz: *Les Troyens* (1863)

Lasting around five hours, Berlioz's epic has it all – stirring drama, battles, romance and a wooden horse. The Greeks take Troy and the Trojan leader Aeneas escapes to Carthage, where the queen, Dido, falls for him. But Aeneas is a man with a mission and leaves her to reclaim his homeland. This one doesn't end well either.

Knockout moment: *'Nuit d'ivresse et d'extase infinie'* ('Night of intoxication and infinite ecstasy') – a love duet for Dido and Aeneas.

Georges Bizet: *Carmen* (1875)

The eponymous Gypsy temptress seduces then rejects the weak-willed soldier Don José, whose life falls apart. Bizet didn't live long enough to see the global domination of his greatest work; today it's the second-most-performed opera in the world.

Knockout moment: Hard to choose because *Carmen* is packed full of memorable melodies – but the rousing *Toreador Song*, sung by the bullfighter Escamillo, is hard to beat.

Benjamin Britten: *Peter Grimes* (1945)

An intensely dramatic tale of a tormented, mis-understood fisherman at odds with his close-knit community, *Grimes* is a twentieth-century master-piece, and the first great English opera to be written in more than two centuries.

Knockout moment: As a contrast to the often intense vocal writing, superbly atmospheric orches-tral *Four Sea Interludes* pepper the score.

Gaetano Donizetti: *L'elisir d'amore* (1832)

The most performed of Donizetti's operas is the story of a simple peasant, Nemorino, in love with wealthy landowner Adina. She's not interested so he blows all his money on a fake 'elixir of love'. When it fails he decides to join the army, an act that finally wins her over.

Knockout moment: *'Una furtiva lagrima'* ('A single furtive tear'), a *cavatina* sung by Nemorino when he believes the love potion is working.

George Gershwin: *Porgy and Bess* (1935)

Porgy depicts life, love and loss on Catfish Row, a poor waterfront neighbourhood in South Carolina.

Knockout moment: Brimming with songs that have also become jazz and pop standards, *Porgy*'s best-loved aria is *'Summertime'*.

Christoph Willibald Gluck: *Orfeo ed Euridice* (1762)

Orfeo misses his dead wife Euridice so much that he is allowed into Hades to find her – but on condition he doesn't look at her. She's confused by this and when he gives in on her insistence, she dies again. But the gods are benevolent and reunite the two once more.

Knockout moment: *'Che farò senza Euridice'* ('What will I do without Euridice?'), in which the grief-stricken Orfeo wonders how he'll cope after his beloved dies for the second time.

Charles Gounod: *Faust* (1859)

An ageing scientist sells his soul to the devil and becomes a virile young man again intent on winning over the lovely Marguerite. But Faust accidentally kills her brother; she goes crazy and murders her child. Faust is dragged to hell as Marguerite heads for the gallows.

Knockout moment: *'Ah, je ris de me voir'* ('Ah, I laugh to see myself') – known as the *Jewel Song*, sung by Marguerite when she finds a box of jewels from Faust left on her doorstep.

George Frideric Handel: *Xerxes* (1738)

King Xerxes is engaged to Amastris, but has fallen in love with Romilda. She, however, is in love with Xerxes' brother. Xerxes gets up to all sorts of shenanigans to remove his rival, but the others are cleverer at plotting and get the better of him.

Knockout moment: *'Ombra mai fu'* ('Never was a shade') – *Xerxes'* opening aria is sung by Xerxes admiring the shade of a plane tree.

Engelbert Humperdinck: *Hänsel und Gretel* (1893)

Two put-upon children are sent to the woods to pick strawberries but they lose their way. They find a gingerbread house where a wicked witch imprisons Hansel with the intention of fattening him up to eat. But the children trick the witch and literally give her a good roasting.

Knockout moment: The *'Abendsegen'* ('Evening Prayer') from the opera's second act, when the children have sand sprinkled into their eyes to send them to sleep.

Franz Lehár: *The Merry Widow* (1905)

The state of Pontevedria is on the verge of going bankrupt and Anna, the widow of the title, must be lured into marrying a Pontevedrian husband so her inheritance stays in the country. With romance and drama all delightfully whipped up into a Viennese trifle, it is today the most performed operetta around the word.

Knockout moment: The *Vilia Song*, about an alluring forest sprite, performed by Anna at a Pontevedrian garden party at her house.

Ruggero Leoncavallo: *I Pagliacci* (1892)

In this famous short opera – often paired with *Cavalleria rusticana* (see below) – adultery and jealousy break out in a travelling theatre company where they're all at it backstage. It climaxes with a murder in front of the audience, blurring the boundaries between the drama and reality.

Knockout moment: *'Vesti la giubba'* ('On with the motley') – in which Canio puts on his clown costume as Pagliaccio to make the audience laugh despite his misery.

Pietro Mascagni: *Cavalleria rusticana* (1890)

The twenty-six-year-old Mascagni won an opera composition contest with this short one-act *verismo* work. He went on to write another fifteen operas but none were so successful. It's the story of passion and betrayal set in Sicily – where else? – at Easter time.

Knockout moment: The sublime *Intermezzo* – a short piece of instrumental music used by Mascagni to mark the passage of time.

Jules Massenet: *Manon* (1884)

One of the most popular French operas. Manon is on her way to a convent when she meets des Grieux and they elope. It's downhill all the way from then on, with Manon eventually being condemned to be deported as a prostitute.

Knockout moment: *'Adieu, notre petite table'* – perhaps the only farewell aria in opera sung to a table, as Manon bids farewell to her humble domestic life.

Claudio Monteverdi: *L'Orfeo* (1607)

The earliest work on this list, *L'Orfeo* was in fact the first great opera. But it was never performed between its premiere and the early twentieth century. It is the familiar story of Orpheus going into Hades to rescue his deceased beloved Euridice.

Knockout moment: Orpheus enters Hades singing *'Possente spirto'* ('Mighty spirit') – highly florid music composed for Monterverdi's star singer, Francesco Rasi.

Wolfgang Amadeus Mozart: *The Marriage of Figaro* (1786)

Mozart at his absolute best gives us depth of character, wit, intrigue and brilliantly complex musical invention. Figaro wants to marry Susanna, but their boss – the Count – attempts to have his way with her first, exercising his rights as lord of the manor.

Knockout moment: Apart from the wonderful Overture, vocal highlights include the divine '*Sull'aria*' ('On the breeze') duet, later used to great effect in the film *The Shawshank Redemption*.

Wolfgang Amadeus Mozart: *The Magic Flute* (1791)

The fourth-most-performed opera in recent years. Mozart's *Singspiel* is a pantomime filled with masonic imagery and meaning, mixing up intense drama and a ludicrous plot.

Knockout moment: *'Der Hölle Rache'* ('Hell's vengeance') – the Queen of the Night's ear-blistering aria with its extraordinarily tricky top Fs.

Modest Mussorgsky: *Boris Godunov* (1869)

Mussorgsky's hugely influential and only completed opera is more about Russian life itself than the tsar who gives the opera its name. The self-taught composer obeyed no accepted rules of dramatic form and created a masterpiece.

Knockout moment: The Death Scene. By the end of the opera, Boris is tortured by guilt and hallucinations. He calls in his son to give him his final counsel.

Jacques Offenbach: *The Tales of Hoffmann* (1881)

Offenbach had seen *The Fantastic Tales of Hoffmann* at the theatre and took five of the stories to turn into his masterpiece. He spent years working on the piece, only to die while it was still in rehearsal.

Knockout moment: The lilting Barcarolle, *'Belle nuit, ô nuit d'amour'* ('Beautiful night, o night of love') is the opera's most famous number.

Sergei Prokofiev: *War and Peace* (1959)

Prokofiev worked on his adaptation of Tolstoy's epic novel for years, starting in the summer of 1942. It wasn't until seventeen years later, following many revisions, and six years after the composer's death, that the full version received its premiere. The opera has more than sixty singing roles but somehow

Prokofiev manages to focus on a few characters and maintain a strong dramatic thread.

Knockout moment: The final scene as Prokofiev whips up a musical snowstorm with harps, piccolos, and tremulous strings.

Giacomo Puccini: *La bohème* (1896)

The world's third-most-performed opera shows scenes of Bohemian life endured by a group of friends in Paris. Love, loss, rivalry and the obligatory consumptive heroine ravish the ears and jerk the tears.

Knockout moment: Another opera with too many hits to choose from. Try *'Che gelida manina'* ('Your tiny hand is frozen') for starters.

Giacomo Puccini: *Madama Butterfly* (1904)

A heartless American naval officer marries an impressionable Japanese geisha girl, then deserts her. But she lives in hope he'll return to her and their child, of whose existence he is unaware.

Knockout moment: *'Un bel di'*, ('One fine day'). Butterfly's heartrending aria, yearning for Pinkerton's return.

Giacomo Puccini: *Turandot* (1926)

Puccini's great unfinished opera – he died while composing the final act – features one huge hit and some of the composer's finest orchestral writing. An ice-cold Chinese princess makes her suitors answer three questions. If they fail, she has them killed. Prince Calaf, however, succeeds.

Knockout moment: The most famous aria – perhaps of them all – is *'Nessun dorma!'* ('None shall sleep') sung by Calaf, proud of his victory in solving Turandot's riddles.

Giacomo Puccini: *Tosca* (1900)

Tosca, a passionate soprano, will go to any lengths to get her imprisoned lover – the painter Cavaradossi – released from the clutches of the evil Baron Scarpia.

Knockout moment: *'Vissi d'Arte'* ('I have lived for art') – Tosca's appeal to Scarpia to release Cavaradossi, stating that she has lived only for art and love.

Henry Purcell: *Dido and Aeneas* (1689)

Purcell premiered his opera at Josias Priest's Boarding School for Girls in Chelsea. Despite its inauspicious start, it has come to be seen as the first great English opera, perhaps the greatest of all time.

Knockout moment: *'When I am laid in earth'* – a beautiful, melancholic aria perhaps unsurpassed in all opera, certainly all English opera.

Gioachino Rossini: *The Barber of Seville* (1816)

Rossini took a risk by setting a story that was already a popular opera by Giovanni Paisiello. But his genius turned the public around and relegated Paisiello's version to obscurity. Delightful all round.

Knockout moment: *'Largo al factotum'* ('Here comes the factotum') – Figaro's calling card is one of opera's most famous moments with its multiple repetitions of the protagonist's name.

Camille Saint-Saëns: *Samson et Dalila* (1877)

An opera dealing with such a racy biblical subject was always going to be a problem for the censors. When it was set to transfer to Covent Garden some thirty years after its original run in Germany, the Lord Chamberlain slapped a ban on it. It contains some of the most beautiful moments in French opera.

Knockout moment: *'Mon coeur s'ouvre à ta voix'* ('Softly awakes my heart') – possibly the finest aria ever written for a mezzo.

Dmitri Shostakovich: *Lady Macbeth of the Mtsensk District* (1934)

The story of a lonely Russian woman who falls in love with one of her husband's workers and is driven to murder. The opera was the vehicle for a general denunciation of Shostakovich's music by the Communist Party in 1936, after being condemned by an anonymous article – sometimes attributed to Stalin himself – in *Pravda*, the Communist Party newspaper.

Knockout moment: The main character's poignant aria *'The foal runs after the filly'*, in Act I scene 3, is the main means by which Shostakovich humanises his heroine. Her downfall is set in motion from then on.

Johann Strauss II: *Die Fledermaus* (1874)

The plot is utterly farcical, focusing on mistaken identity, flirtation and a practical joke that has unforeseen consequences. Its utter accessibility – musically and dramatically – made it a sure-fire hit.

Knockout moment: The Overture is eight minutes packed full of tunes, all of which end up appearing during the course of the action that follows.

Richard Strauss: *Salome* (1905)

In Jerusalem, Salome – stepdaughter of Herod – becomes entranced with the voice of John the Baptist, who is imprisoned in an old well. She wants a kiss from John but he refuses. Herod tells Salome if she dances for him, he will give her what she wants. She dances and requests John's head on a silver platter. She kisses it and Herod has her killed.

Knockout moment: The Dance of the Seven Veils, in which Salome usually sheds all her clothes after dancing for more than ten minutes, and then sings a long monologue.

Richard Strauss: *Der Rosenkavalier* (1911)

This sumptuous, elegant grand ball of an opera was one of Richard Strauss's biggest successes. An incredibly rich score.

Knockout moment: The closing *'Ist ein traum'* ('Is it a dream?') are among the most ecstatic moments you'll ever hear in opera.

Igor Stravinsky: *The Rake's Progress* (1951)

Based loosely on a series of engravings by Hogarth, which Stravinsky had seen in a Chicago exhibition, the story concerns the decline and fall of Tom Rakewell, who deserts Anne Trulove for the delights of London in the company of Nick Shadow, who turns out to be the Devil.

Knockout moment: *'No word from Tom'* – Rakewell's beloved Anne yearns to hear from him.

Pyotr Ilyich Tchaikovsky: *Eugene Onegin* (1879)

Tatyana believes the handsome, unconventional and selfish Onegin is the man of her dreams. He lives to regret his rejection of her and his incitement of a duel in which his best friend dies.

Knockout moment: The Polonaise. *Onegin* rivals Tchaikovsky's greatest ballets with its stupendous, orchestral dance music.

Giuseppe Verdi: *Rigoletto* (1851)

One of the greatest and most darkly dramatic of all operas. Rigoletto, a court jester, has a secret daughter, Gilda. She, though, has fallen for his boss, the salacious Duke. Rigoletto plots to have the Duke killed but it all goes terribly wrong.

Knockout moment: *'La donna è mobile'* ('Woman is fickle') is one of the great tenor showpieces. Verdi knew it was going to be a huge hit and kept the aria under wraps until opening night.

Giuseppe Verdi: *La traviata* (1853)

After a disappointing premiere, Verdi said, 'Future generations will appreciate this opera.' He was right – it is now the world's most performed opera. Alfredo falls for courtesan Violetta. She agrees to live with him but his father pressures her to break up the relationship with tragic consequences.

Knockout moment: The *Drinking Song* (*'Libiamo ne lieti calici'*) is an all-time favourite, although not typical of the mood of the rest of *La traviata*.

Giuseppe Verdi: *Aida* (1871)

An Ethiopian princess, Aida, is being held captive as a slave in Egypt. She and Egyptian General Radames are in love. But when he is appointed supreme commander against Ethiopia, she is deeply conflicted about her love for her country and for him.

Knockout moment: The *'Grand March'* welcomes the triumphant Radames back to Egypt. Expect real horses, lots of armour and maybe even an elephant or two.

Richard Wagner: *Tristan und Isolde* (1865)

Tristan is a Cornish knight who has captured an Irish princess to deliver to his king. But Tristan and Isolde fall in love on the journey, helped along by a magic love potion.

Knockout moment: The stunning *Liebestod* ('Love's death') is sung at the end of the opera by Isolde over Tristan's dead body.

Richard Wagner: *Parsifal* (1882)

Wagner described *Parsifal* not as an opera, but as a 'Festival Play for the Consecration of the Stage'. The knight Parsifal must rescue the stolen spear that pierced Jesus on the cross, overcoming various temptations along the way.

Knockout moment: The *'Good Friday Music'* from the third act, depicting nature as a manifestation of God's love.

Carl Maria von Weber: *Der Freischütz* (1821)

The first important German Romantic opera was a big influence on Wagner. Max must fire a successful shot in order to prove himself worthy to marry the head forester's daughter. A mate who has sold his soul to the 'black huntsman' persuades Max to meet him in the Wolf's Glen to cast magic bullets. The next day, Max's last magic bullet unfortunately hits the girl.

Knockout moment: The famous Wolf's Glen scene has been described as 'the most expressive rendering of the gruesome that is to be found in a musical score'.

seven

The Top 30 Opera Tracks to Download

Here's a list of thirty of the most popular operatic pieces ever written – works that almost always feature in the annual Classic FM Hall of Fame, the top 300 chart of favourite classical tracks voted for by listeners. You can find them as a downloadable playlist on our website at ClassicFM.com/handyguides

Bellini, *Norma*: 'Casta diva'

Maria Callas made this aria her own for generations of opera lovers, although today it has been claimed by a number of other singers, including Cecilia Bartoli.

Bizet, *Carmen: Habanera*

The Habanera is the popular name for the aria *'L'amour est un oiseau rebelle'* ('Love is a rebellious bird') with which the sultry character of Carmen makes her entrance.

Bizet, *Carmen: Toreador Song*

The bullfighter Escamillo gives us one of opera's greatest songs and a new word. Not satisfied with the correct term *torero*, Bizet invented the four-syllable *toreador* to fit his musical plan.

Bizet, *The Pearl Fishers: 'Au fond du temple saint'*

Bizet's opera is almost solely remembered for this outstanding duet, sung by two friends caught in a love triangle with the same girl.

Britten, *Peter Grimes: Four Sea Interludes*

Britten paints such powerful and vivid images in music of the power of the sea and the elements and their impact on a Suffolk coastal fishing town.

Delibes, *Lakmé: Flower Duet*

After it appeared in a British Airways commercial in 1989, this beautiful duet became one of the most well-known pieces of classical music. Few, however, have seen the opera it comes from.

Dvořák, *Rusalka*: *Song to the Moon*

This beautiful melody is a water nymph's prayer, asking the moon to illuminate her love for a prince she has seen by the lake.

Gluck, *Orfeo ed Euridice*: 'Che faro'

Orpheus laments the loss of his beloved in this poignant aria from Gluck's revolutionary opera.

Handel, *Xerxes*: 'Ombra mai fu'

One of Handel's best-known and most loved works, this sublime aria is best sung by a countertenor rather than a soprano.

Mascagani, *Cavalleria rusticana*: *Intermezzo*

One of the single most attractive tunes in all opera – an orchestral interlude that has also been put to use in movies, such as *Raging Bull* and *The Godfather Part III*.

Massenet, *Thaïs*: *Meditation*

An intermezzo written for violin and orchestra from

this otherwise little-known opera. The Meditation has become a popular encore for violinists and other instrumentalists.

Mozart, *Così fan tutte*: *'Soave sia il vento'*
Two sisters wish safe travels to their soldier suitors, unaware that a plot has been hatched to test the girls' fidelity.

Mozart, *The Magic Flute*: *'Der Hölle Rache'*
Stand by for vocal gymnastics. Mozart wrote the Queen of the Night's famous aria for his sister-in-law Josepha and her striking, naturally high *coloratura* voice.

Mozart, *The Marriage of Figaro*: *Overture*
This scintillating, scurrying Overture, to be played very fast, is as big a hit in the concert hall as in the opera house.

Mozart, *The Marriage of Figaro*: *'Sull'aria'*
Countess Almaviva dictates to her maid Susanna an invitation to a tryst designed to expose the Count's infidelity. Stupid, but absolutely sublime.

Verdi, *Aida*: *Grand March*

It doesn't get much grander than this. Verdi even commissioned a unique, straight trumpet to be created to make the victorious sound he wanted.

Verdi, *La traviata*: *Drinking Song*

Raise your glasses in this rumbustious toast that launches Verdi's tragic tale of doomed love. It's downhill all the way from here.

Verdi, *Nabucco*: *'Va pensiero'*

The text for the *Chorus of the Hebrew Slaves* was the first thing that captured Verdi's attention when he read the libretto for *Nabucco*. It has remained one of his most popular tunes.

Wagner, *Die Walküre*: *Ride of the Valkyries*

The second of Wagner's four-opera *Ring* Cycle gives us this thundering tune, much loved by filmmakers, from Francis Ford Coppola to the creators of Bugs Bunny.

Wagner, *Tannhäuser*: *Pilgrim's Chorus*

The perfect depiction of a solemn religious journey, Wagner's pilgrims seem to emerge out of the distance, pass by and then disappear on their way again.

Wagner, *Tristan und Isolde*: *Liebestod*
Wagner's tale of the 'bliss and wretchedness of love' could end only with one 'sole redemption – death'. But boy, does it sound beautiful.

eight

Useful Operatic Terms

aria A solo song that usually expresses what the character is feeling or thinking.

Baroque era The period from around 1600 to 1750, which included such composers as Bach, Vivaldi and Handel, who championed new genres including the concerto and the sonata.

bel canto Literally 'beautiful singing' – a vocal style that puts the emphasis on the range of the voice, quality of tone and ornamentation.

cabaletta The animated second section of an aria in nineteenth-century Italian opera, following an initial songlike *cantabile*. It often introduces a complication in the plot.

castrato A male singer, with a surgically created

high voice, who took the part of a woman in seventeenth-century Italian operas.

Classical era   The period that started around 1750, when composers such as Haydn, Mozart, Beethoven and Rossini were writing music.

cavatina   A simple, languid, melodious song.

coloratura   A female voice, required to sing elaborate music with trills, scales and incredibly high notes.

coup de théâtre   A theatrical trick staged for dramatic effect.

continuo   The bass line of music, often on a harpsichord, that underpins the melody.

diva   Literally, 'goddess' – usually applied to a soprano possessed of exceptional talent and a possibly demanding nature.

duet   A song sung by two singers together.

grand opera   Spectacular theatrical events combining music, large casts and even animals on stage.

leitmotif   A passage of music, pioneered by Wagner, that represents a particular character, place or idea.

libretto   The words or text for an opera, written by a librettist.

melodrama   An especially thrilling stage work in

which the music intensifies the effect of the drama. Also a work where words are interspersed with music.

neoclassical A twentieth-century movement in which composers tried to return to Classicism, in their approach to order, style and emotional restraint.

opera buffa Italian comic operas with an emphasis on patter and clever wordplay.

opera seria Italian serious opera based on grand heroic or mythological themes.

operetta Light opera pioneered by Offenbach and taken up by Viennese composers.

recitative The part of the text, echoing speech patterns, that moves the plot along.

Romantic era The period that began around 1830 and ended around 1900 in which music became less formal and increasingly expressive and inventive.

Score The written music notating how all the vocal and instrumental parts should be sung and played.

Singspiel German-language music drama with spoken dialogue, interspersed by ensemble songs and arias.

surtitles   The opera's text displayed as it is being sung, on a screen above the stage.

through-composed   A style of opera consisting of an uninterrupted stream of music, as opposed to having songs interspersed with recitative and dialogue.

verismo   A realistic and often darkly dramatic style of opera, drawing on real life, contemporary stories.

About Classic FM

If this series of books has whetted your appetite to find out more, one of the best ways to discover what you like about classical music is to listen to Classic FM. We broadcast a huge breadth of classical music 24 hours a day across the UK on 100–102 FM, on DAB digital radio, online at ClassicFM.com, on Sky Channel 0106, on Virgin Media channel 922 and on FreeSat channel 721. You can also download the free Classic FM App, which will enable you to listen to Classic FM on your iPhone, iPod, iPad, Blackberry or Android device.

As well as being able to listen online, you will find a host of interactive features about classical music, composers and musicians on our website, ClassicFM.com. When we first turned on Classic FM's transmitters more than two decades ago, we changed the face of classical music radio in the UK for ever. Now, we are doing the same online.

The very best way to find out more about which pieces of classical music you like is by going out and hearing a live performance by one of our great British orchestras for yourself. There is simply no substitute for seeing the whites of the eyes of a talented soloist as he or she performs a masterpiece on stage only a few feet in front of you, alongside a range of hugely accomplished musicians playing together as one.

Classic FM has a series of partnerships with orchestras across the country: the Bournemouth Symphony Orchestra, the London Symphony Orchestra, the Orchestra of Opera North, the Philharmonia Orchestra, the Royal Liverpool Philharmonic Orchestra, the Royal Northern Sinfonia and the Royal Scottish National Orchestra. And don't forget the brilliant young musicians of the National Children's Orchestra of Great Britain and of the National Youth Orchestra of Great Britain. To see if any of these orchestras have a concert coming up near you, log onto our website at ClassicFM. com and click on the 'Concerts and Events' section. It will also include many other classical concerts – both professional and amateur – that are taking place near where you live.

Happy listening!

About the Author

Rob Weinberg is the On Air Editor of Classic FM Interactive, the online platform of Global's national classical music station, Classic FM. After graduating with a degree in Expressive Arts from Brighton Polytechnic in 1987, Rob began his career in local radio newsrooms around the UK. He joined Classic FM as a Producer in 1994. Among his proudest achievements are producing Classic FM's six-part centenary series on William Walton with Humphrey Burton; the exclusive UK broadcast of *The Three Tenors at Wembley*; *Ken Russell's Movie Classics*; *The Muppets' Classic Christmas*, presented by Kermit the Frog; *Music – A Joy for Life* with Sir Edward Heath; the first performance at the Royal Albert Hall of Paul McCartney's *Standing Stone*; and the world premiere of Walt Disney Pictures' *Fantasia 2000*. He produced Classic FM's opera show from 1994 to 2007.

Index

Index

In the same series